Rising, Falling, All of Us

New and Collected Poems
by

Thelma T. Reyna

OTHER BOOKS BY THELMA T. REYNA

The Heavens Weep for Us and Other Stories (2009)

Breath & Bone (2011; poetry)

Hearts in Common (2013; poetry)

First Edition
Golden Foothills Press

PRAISE FOR THE POETRY OF THELMA T. REYNA

Hearts in Common (2013)

"The poems...crisscross between cultures and genders. Thelma T. Reyna creates a lattice work of...who we are as a nation—the land of the many. Reyna also reminds the reader that we all have universal needs for love and acceptance, and likewise, we all feel the same pain of loss and rejection. Reyna's poetry is heartfelt and powerful."

--Leah Maines, Award-Winning Poet
Editor & Publisher, Finishing Line Press

Breath & Bone (2011)

"These poems are songs of survival. The breath in this collection is baby's breath, lover's breath, mother's breath, the spirit of stars and silence, the dust of Texas roads. The bones are the bones of memory, old blankets, empty bottles and the sleeping bags of homeless vets. ...Thelma T. Reyna gathers her breath and bone into one strong voice that testifies to the healing power of telling the truth."

--Cassie Premo Steele, Ph.D.
Award-Winning Poet

"Thelma Reyna explores the terrain of moments, some physical, some emotional, some symbolic. Her mapping of this topography is both lyrical and tactile,...identifiable and transcendent at the same time. Thelma's language suggests the natural world, while it brings out a wide expanse of human experience from birth to death, with material poverty and emotional wealth being central aspects of her characters' landscapes."

--Annmarie Lockhart
Award-Winning Poet
Founding Editor, Vox Poetica

"*Breath & Bone* confronts rewarding passions and others painful on the page. An admirable boldness to this chapbook."

--Pat Mora
Award-Winning Poet

"Reyna's poetry is a collection of daguerreotype photographs: haunting, timeless, well-crafted. Each poem brings the reader into a definitive moment in time, the moments revealed by just enough light to remain both mysterious and obscure and to remind the reader that a real human being is speaking through the verse. Sincerity is her strength. Reyna keeps gorgeous poetry alive, every phrase perfectly placed and laced with big moments of wow."

--Lisa Marie Basile
Award-Winning Poet
Editor of Caper Literary Journal
Editor of Vwa: Voices of Haiti

To the memory of the first published poet in our family history:
Mercedes Cortez Téllez.

To my beloved family, for whom I toil and try to tell our stories.

ACKNOWLEDGMENTS

The following poems first appeared in a prior version in the following publications:

- In the author's poetry chapbook, *Breath & Bone* (Finishing Line Press, 2011):
  The Morning After; Spoons; Quilts; Annie's Lap; Growing Up Dusty in a Small Texas Town; On Loan; Grandmother's Insomnia; Degas; On January 1st, the Glass Slipper Won't Fit; Last Rites; Monster Lady (formerly titled How She Died); Jumper; Flight 93: September 11, 2001; Iconoclast; Sylvia Plath's Fingers; Romeo & Juliet: How It Could've Been; After the Final Act.

- In the author's poetry chapbook, *Hearts in Common* (Finishing Line Press, 2013):
  Poet with Braids; Estero Beach, Baja California; Crickets; Rainy Day in 'Nam (formerly titled Rainy Day in 'Nam: My Brother Danny, 1968); To My 12-Year-Old Daughter; Sleepless Night; Haiti 3: Belly Fat; Call Me; How Could You Have Done This?; Mi Amor; Clutter, Mental Clutter; What Do I Race Against?; Tahrir Square, Cairo: January 27, 2011; Do Not Resuscitate; To Mercedes in Laredo: An 88-Year-Old Poet; This I Know.

- In *San Gabriel Valley Poets Quarterly*, in various issues/years as indicated:
  Brown Arms (Spring 2011); School Bell (Summer 2011); Chicago Winter People (Fall 2011); Manicure Diva: Hong Hanh, Apricot Blossom (Winter 2012); Early Morning (Spring 2012); Coming to Empty (Summer 2012); Shades of Blue (Fall 2012); Oscar the Blade Runner (Winter 2013); Old Habits (Spring, 2013); To Vanessa (Summer 2013); Janus the Gateway God (Fall 2013); It's Midnight (Winter 2014).

- In *Free Love 2 Anthology,* February 2014:
  Stone Hearts

- In *Poetry & Cookies Anthology of Poems,* in various years as indicated:
  Chicago Poem #2: Hammock: Chicago Old Town [originally titled, "Hammock: Chicago Old Town"] (2012); Rosita's Hands (2012); Talismans (2013); I Stopped by Your House (2013); Flying Home (2014); Crossings (2014).

- In *Journal of Modern Poetry [JOMP],* Volume 16 (2013):
  Chicago Rain; To Charles Bukowski: About Poems.

- In the literary magazine, *If & When:*
  The Undivorced (May 2013).

- In the *SGVP Calendar Issue,* in the years as indicated:
  Awake (2011); The Mayans Were Wrong (2012).

- In the online *Caper Literary Journal, www.CaperLitJournal.com:*
  By the L.A. Freeway (August 4, 2010).

- In the anthology, *Vwa: Voices of Haiti* (2010):
  Haiti 1: Burials (originally titled, "Burials"); Haiti 2: A Drought of Tears (originally titled, "A Drought of Tears").

- In *The Altadena Review* (Summer 1984):
  Grumpy: The Untold Story

- In the textbook, *New Voices in Language, Literature, and Composition: 1* (1978):
  Revuelto Con Arroz (Mixed with Rice).

- Cover photo from 123RF.com; (123RF USA): San Francisco, CA.
- Cover designed by Dominic Gilormini in South Pasadena, CA.

TABLE OF CONTENTS

Part I: Rising...

Part II: Falling...

Part III: ...All of Us

I

Rising...

TO CHARLES BUKOWSKI:
ABOUT POEMS

"if [a poem] doesn't come bursting out of you...
if it never does roar out of you...
unless it comes out of your soul like a rocket...
don't do it...."
--Charles Bukowski,
"So You Want to Be a Writer"

mine sometimes trickle out like drops of blood from wounds not
sealed, steady plops of purple that stain the page while fingers
tremble at ancient recollections

mine swim in dreams, mixing with clouds and stars and truncated
faces, with feathers and angels and mothers long gone, and
swirl uncertain in stews set at tables like yours

mine slip soundless from the womb with forceps near, just in
case, just in case, and gather voice with warmth and
light and arms that welcome and embrace

mine toddle to daylight with thumb plugged in, hope taking
my words on infant legs to journeys near and far, stumbling
on hills and stones but pushing on

POPE FRANCIS

Where have you been all our lives,
holy man? Rock star, they say, but others
say slummer, slinking into blackness in
Argentina's ghettos, wafting without
fanfare into dying rooms, holding
calloused hands and emaciated
faces breathing their last. Plodding in
your orthopedic shoes through cobblestones
and dirt, through doorways hid in trash, with
only pinpoint stars as witness to your
mercy. The least of these, people of
dust under politicians' heels, are
Christ to you, and you to them.

You dared take this clarity to Rome, to
palaces putrid with gilt and guilt, to
hallways ancient with greed and god, where
men of the cloth wear silk and tassels
touting themselves. You wash weary pilgrims'
feet, kiss faces deformed, and recount your
sins to the world. What window burst open
in heaven to release you to earth, what
wisdom exploded in the watching gods to
awake and understand and send us you?

The planets spin eternal in cycles, with suns
and moons in orbits keeping frigid skies
alight, but you, holy man, have wracked earth with
tremors upending the centuries, cataclysms that
sunder egoists and plutocrats and knock them
off pedestals they pilfered. You, holy man,
are us, and we are you, and god is you, and
we are god.

—   —

POET WITH BRAIDS

Like docile snakes, your braids lie thick,
blackness glossy and knotted to your waist. Your
tendril beard and sideburns shock
when you raise your face
and show the world that you're a man:

poet man, brown poet from maya-land, glorified
in rhyme stilted with accents raw, words
that stumble on furling tongue, that catch
sometimes to tell the world you came from
jungles misted in centuries of mystery and loss.

Brown poet with braids, caramel fingers
slender on pencil songs, soul enwrapped in
other times, pyramid stones, and blood
curling its way down massive steps
where giants worshipped sun and death.

Brown poet man, gentle snakes on back,
face intent in this new land, dreams binding
distant lores and newfound shores, eyes seeing
things unseen by fathers buried deep.

SCHOOL BELL

The school-child, all pudgy knees
and dimpled hands, holds close communion
with a polished beetle in the grass.

His knapsack lists on the emerald sea of dew.
Pillow fingers poke the creature, its
itinerary a graver concern to the
tardy scholar than school is.

The child's laughter tinkles in the corner of
the yard, while children scurry like lemmings
at the ringing of the bell.
Alone, entranced, the solitary
child and iridescent bug meet and confer, enwrapped
in one another's charms:
so full of promised evolution,
 so small and at the mercy of the world,
compatriots oblivious to
books and clocks
and all that bind.

THE MORNING AFTER

Last night the virile wind, his massive chest puffed with
       braggadocio, wrestled briefly with the
       rain before his loins overpowered her,

and the universe stood witness to orgiastic throes—
       weepings, thrashings, ululations, convulsions
       of copulation in the heavens,

and this glassene morning is the child born, with
       lacquered sidewalks showing undersides of
       leaves, lapis skies shaking off their mists, icing dripping
       down the sides of steaming mountains, and
       trees, naked yet in mucus-birth, quivering
       skinnily in their babyfrost.

MINI-EROTICA: A HAIKU SEQUENCE

I

glistening bodies
our pubes glazed with jism
mattress moist at dawn

II

I buck against your
heaviness, eyes shut; blood rush-
es like white water

III

you tap my finger
in the hollow of my throat:
tree well filled with sweat

IV

we glide from one an-
other; I feather-rub my
hands across your thighs

GRANDMOTHER'S INSOMNIA

She awaits daylight on the skinny edge of
her daughter's cot, rolled
away in mornings, at night a rusty
sentry in the spidered corner of the hall.
Like a wax figure melting, she sinks to
her knees, now permanently ahed from
prayer, her paper lips whispering the
Credo, Ave Maria, and a hundred holy
lines she can mouth in sleep—if sleep comes—her
knobby fingers twined like vines, wooden rosary
swaying from her palms.

After eighty years, day and night meld into
one. Closeness to eternity makes
blackness deep and long. Her feather body
wafts from room to room, gloom
to gloom, prickly shawl cocooning her from
drafts. She peeks on tiptoes at the sleeping, slumps
beside the stove, flames long-dead, passes to the
parlor, where moonlight cuts long shadows in
the rug and frames her narrow face as
she lifts the curtain from the pane
and peers outside
again.

SPOONS

You gather me into a fetus in your arms
and we lie front to back
like spoons
in these sleepless embryo hours
front to back
like spoons.

I lift myself against the hottest part of you
to fit myself against your throb
your brown arms shield my lilting pulse
crisscross my breasts and fuse
my heat with yours.

Your muscled thighs push mine
your lips open like a nursing babe's
leave silver on my nape.
I push harder against you
like spoons.

ESTERO BEACH, BAJA CALIFORNIA

melted-butter sun by six
                    morning haze a whisper by pink
          breakwaters   last night's foot-

     prints smudged along geranium-
               bordered walks   white
                    stones piled to mark *la zona peligrosa*

TO MY 12-YEAR-OLD DAUGHTER

Your limbs are long and sleek, umbre skin glistening in
moonlight, womanbreasts quivering shyly as you turn
and resettle into dreams.

My heart stammers to alchemize your rounded
flesh into angles and knobbiness of childhood. I
tiptoed in tonight, as I've done since first you left *my* breast,
my arms that blocked away the world so long, my
hands that tucked blankets, my lips that brushed your
child-brow, your filigree lashes long and twined with
tendril wisps of glossy black.

A million midnights I've peeked in, padded feet marking a
pilgrim's path to your side. And yet, until tonight, my
mother-eyes saw *child*, a fragile ball encamped beneath the
sheets, twig knees at times escaping from the warmth. My muffled
footsteps counted off the months, but my heart remained
transfixed in infant years.

I smooth the coverlet around your feet, anoint these with
a gentle kiss. Sadness swells my heart to know you're
farther now, farther on the path that grows away
from me, farther on the path that grows wider
into brush unseen, farther on the path
that will split your life
from mine someday.

FLYING HOME

You're flying home, my daughter, wrapped in
      down, white wisps of wool around your neck
      protecting you from snow and winds that
      wait for you two thousand miles hence.
How many times you've crossed these clouds!

Proud bird, beautiful bird that flew my california
      coop and stretched your wings to broader skies,
      strong bird breaking free, braving sleet and ice
      and all that slips.
Proud bird flying home again, to your own nest,
      your mate and birdlings hunkered in straw
      frazzled with missing you.

Mother birds are tough. We see our nests go empty
      when the shaping's done, the gathering and
      fitting of twigs and leaves and bits of lint. We
      clawed predators away, spread feathers over
      nestling eyes sealed shut, fed you with our
      mouth, kept you warm.
But mother birds are tough. We push you farther
      to the edge and cast you to the air, to see your
      wings take flight, to soar you closer to the sun.
We see our nests go empty and weep.

Mother birds are tough, you and I. Someday you'll
      gift the skies with yours, tossing frail feathers
      and legs into the blue and watching, heart in
      throat.
Your bursting pride in seeing them ascend will block
      the pain of watching them vanish into clouds.

BROWN ARMS

He doesn't know I watch, or
maybe yes, he does. He carries rocks
in arms burnt browner by the sun, in arms
sinewed and knotted by muscles stretching and
pushing against granite edges of patio
pavers he lays in puzzles beyond my ken.

Sweat veneers his back like varnish freshly
stroked. His knees straddle opened earth, leather hands cupping
moistness as he digs deeper, smoothing loam, opening the
hole, plunging fingers into dirt made soft with rain. Face lowered,
droplets of his labor anoint the bed.

He hardly rests. He sips from plastic cups I bring to
him with eyes averted from the truth. His dark fingers brush
my wrist, a moment pardoned with a flush, and he
turns to toil that defines his being. Hour after
hour, in days long with longing, his brown arms lift
and move and hold and carry and embrace.

What does he think while his muscles groan, sweat
salting his lips and nipples as it trickles to
his pants? I lean against the wall, curtain falling
closed again, my knees useless.

ROSITA'S HANDS

Rosita's hands soaked in early morning suds,
the scalding pinking her skin as she
swooshed and swirled the scouring pad and
scrubbed pans until they sparkled.

Then her prune-skin hands wiped baby's
face, peach oatmeal sticking on Allegra's
chin and rosebud mouth, dangling like mushy
earrings on the child's pale curls as she
cooed and grabbed for Rosita's Gerber wipe.

At noon, Rosita's hands folded linens with
precision, her fingers pressing creases in lines
straight and pure, stacking sheets and cases in
the master rooms while baby dreamt of
dolls and Rosita dreamt of vows.

At four, Rosita's hands waved to Allegra and
her mother, gathered car keys and canvas purse, then
lay still on the manicurist's table as her nails were
freed of jagged edges and transformed to
ruby nuggets of promise.

When I raise my hand tonight, Rosita said to
the manicurist, and, smiling, raised her free hand
to demonstrate, *when I take the oath, I want my
hand to be beautiful.* She inhaled radiantly:
*And when I sign the paper at the end, when I sign my
name, my hands will be beautiful.*

Rosita's hands lay on the towel on the table, pristine, the tiny salon fan whirring its breath on the red-tipped hands that tonight, tonight, tonight would be *American* hands at last.

CRICKETS

Crickets detest silence.
They're sirens
with nonstop trills that sunder the summer air
as they tear
me, too. Crickets moan, and I recollect

      sultry Texas nights
      and fights
      with my man under trees in a forsaken park,
      making love while crickets shamed the dark,
      or crying alone on the back porch
      while crickets sang their pity. Worse,

crickets never slept.

SHADOW LOVE

I don't recall when we first spoke. But I
remember how his tall frame ambled by my
table that first time, and he stalled beside my chair, not knowing
I could see his reflection in the glass across the room, and he looked
down on my head and paused as I looked straight
ahead and didn't move. I could hardly breathe. His reflection was so
gorgeous, and the book he carried snagged my heart:
Reading Lolita in Tehran—clash of cultures, one group loving
the other from afar, from the shadows, loving the forbidden,
fearing disaster and braving the chance of
everything falling apart.

He didn't speak to me then, but only after days of pretending not
to see me, and I feigning not to care. There, just feet away, always
sitting near the window, where he could watch my face no
matter where I sat in that cafe. And I saw the thick black coffee
he preferred, the heavy pastries he held lightly in fingers slender and
slow, watched him licking icing from scones, frowning in
his coffee cup, deciphering how he could hear
my breath, miles away.

Our fingers brushed together when we reached for napkins at the
counter's end. *Reading Lolita,* bent, dog-eared, lay on the table
by my hand. He blushed. My blood pulsated in my head
when he spoke and broke the barricade we'd had. His heavy
accent, bumbling words, deep red face—but his gaze
spoke the words that tripped his tongue.
Love at first sight, love from out the shadows, but, as it turned out,
shadow love.

—   —

He was alien, undocumented, illegal. Poems he whispered as we lay
in dusky rooms spoke of love, forgiveness, the preciousness of time,
children's breath, and the loneliness of death. But like the reading of
Lolita, we loved on borrowed time, in stealth and
furtive hours, aware of risks and how
things fall apart.
Love without
papers is
hard.

SLEEPLESS NIGHT

This sleepless night is ours,
to lie side by side,
arms touching tip to tip,
bodies hip to hip,
eyes tracing shadows weaving on the walls.

No words, love, no words,
just toes brushing with the gentlest kiss,
our warmth pressing lip to lip,
blood coursing
to the softest tune.

No words, love, no words.
Just you and me
wrapped up
in solitude and certitude
that this sleepless night is ours.

CALL ME

She runs into old friends, or people she hardly
knows,
boyfriends she dumped, or who dumped her long
ago.
Ersatz smile, gleaming teeth, lips polished super
red,
flirting eyelashes quick to flash, full of things
unsaid.
A hug, a laugh, a story shared in the grocery
aisle,
Hands on hips, hair tossed back: the epitome of
style.

Call me. Pause. *Here's my number.* Laugh. *No,
really!*
Pencil moving, gold rings glowing. *Oh, don't be
silly!*
Bright kiss on his cheek, warm hug on his neck and
arms—
These guys can still respond to
charm.

Decades passed, people came and
went.
She retired, but her time is still well-
spent.
*Yes, yes, call me. My numbers are the
same.*
The girl's still got
game!

CHICAGO POEM #1: WINTER

Winter people, people of parkas, flecked
beards, eyebrows dusted with flakes
and mist, people with necks craned
to concrete slick with mud and slides, ducking
winds that pierce their bones and paralyze.

Winter people, babies swaddled beyond
recognition, lumps of down, acrylic, wool,
zarapes, bunting balled into carriages navigating
walkways perilous with slush and hail, nannies
with eyes squeezed against pummels of chill.

Winter people, homeless men hunkered in
detritus, doorways dark and cramped, army
blankets damp from dew, sneakers brown from dirt,
broken sidewalks chapped by wind and ash, grizzled
lips pressed in prayer found again at last.

Winter people, gathered 'round the open fire
roaring in the parking lot, orange tongues embracing
sticks and crumpled paper sacks thrown in and stoked,
asphalt warmed with embers that light the frozen night,
flames casting shadows gaunt against stone walls.

CHICAGO POEM #2: HAMMOCK, OLD TOWN

How different the world is from here!
I lie in white ropes woven and matted like
an old woman's braids, arms snug at my sides, my
outstretched body still as it sways side
to side, gentle arcs smiling between the porch
rail and the gingko tree.

The sky transforms to green. Leaves from
the colonnade of trees standing guard all 'round
intertwine to create a canopy that breathes
and quivers with each breeze, that shimmies gray
to sage to emerald and lime, brushing on branches
that cross the green expanse like arteries from
the mighty Nile.

I see things unseen: intricate brickwork at the edges
of our roof, four stories tall into clouds that
brush silver-painted gutters and mismatched tiles.
Ceiling rafters on porch stacked on porch. Planter
boxes varying from wood to metal and plastic, painted
black or white, perched up and down on wrought
iron railings like backpacks on soldiers marching
in line.

Skinny buildings rise like pillars of stone and
steel as I glance from side to side. Four stories in each
monolith—filled with stories of humanity—their windows
reflecting shadows and light and the sliding of trees
and wires and things unseen.

The hammock sways me like a babe in arms, like
an infant curled in its mother's breast, eyes wide, eyes
shut, seeing the unseen rock and arc, the body
like a pendulum that soothes.

CHICAGO RAIN

This rain slaps down houses and trees, coats windows
with fat rivulets that glob and tremble.
This rain brawls, kicking roofs and walls,
flexing bully muscles, pounding cars that snake like
dotted lines across asphalt gurgling with foam and brack.

Thunder cracks the sky.
Thunder roars like mythic monsters chained to rocks, their
bellies swollen with ire and hunger.
Deep-throated, full-throttle thunder, rumbles that roil and convulse,
that startle clouds and men.

This thunder and this rain: two sluggers splitting
heaven open like eggs and running amok in
alleys, stirring gutter rats and curling into curbside
puddles too big to breach, into rooster tails too
tall to pass. Chicago hunches its Carl Sandburg
shoulders, braces its sinewed back, and
soldiers on.

STONE HEARTS

I collect them every chance I get, under shrubs dried
from winds that sap life out of things, or in gurgling
streams. Stone hearts buried beneath others like
them, stones misshapen by elements.

I stoop in creeks like miners seeking gold, eyes
scanning gray, white, brown, beige, black stones
arrayed like faces in a crowd—looking for the
right, rounded head cleft in two, with
opposing point that makes a heart a heart. Smooth
rocks that glint in sand, or craggy stones
lying with clods and scorpions and
dung beetles in thorns.

A heart's a heart. Doesn't matter where it
hides or shows itself, how wind and sun and
storms have buffeted or cosseted, how it's been
tossed or laid in moss. I gather these in
pockets by my breast.

MI AMOR
(Take 2)

Our bodies meld in
passion, our pubes glazed
with jism.

we roll away from one
another. I tap my finger in
the hollow of my throat, little
tree-well filled with sweat,

and feather-rub my hands
across your thighs,
my body bursting with summer sun.

LET THERE BE LIGHT

I flood my rooms each daybreak--
slide drapes, lift shades, swing doors to
do the god thing: bring in light.

Outside, the moon's a faded coin
on trees and clouds, an old woman with
her luster stripped who knows and waits.

Inside, the sink streaks gold, rays swathe
stone floors, the cat blinks and slinks down
from the tabletop, sun-blind.

My calendar can't tell me how my day
will go, lauded or denuded, how far my
psyche slides, or if I shine.

But at dawn, my hands are wands
that banish blackness, for it's true: what they
say, about god inside, god in each of us, how

we're
all
god.

II

...Falling...

MANICURE DIVA:
HONG HANH, APRICOT BLOSSOM

When they call her "diva," she ducks her head, her thick hair
      falling like curtains to shield her cheeks.
She looks up only to greet clients or reach for tools she wields
      with grace and skill unmatched in the salon.

Hong Hanh: manicurist extraordinaire, epitome of modesty and
      expertise! her clients rave.
They heap praise upon their diva, petite lady of amber eyes
      and perfect teeth, artist who cuts and trims and
      swooshes and colors and transforms the mundane to
      majestic.
They dip into Calvin Klein and Kate Spade bags for tips to
      stuff into Hong's flowered pockets or press into her
      hand.

But when doors are locked, and
Americans are gone, and
lamplight paints the sidewalks yellow, and
tall glass windows turn black and cold, and
Hong flips the OPEN sign around, and
sweeps the floor in urgent arcs,

a pall hangs in the shop.
Specters float beside her at the sink, as she rinses scissors and
      clippers and fruit for the shrine behind the counter.
Hong Hanh: tiny woman of Saigon fields, of brothers slain in wars
      and sisters enslaved in beds.
Hong Hanh: aborter of two children from rapist monsters.
Hong Hanh: daughter of parents abandoned in a land lost in mist and
      misery.

—

Her hands work magic by day, and pray by night.
Her head bows over hands by day, and bows on the ground by
      night, tears staining photos and rugs and wooden floor.
Her heart lies calm and meek in the salon by day, and flails with
      grief by night,
      each night,
her escape across oceans to freedom unable to free her soul.

GUADALAJARA, GUADALAJARA

My children called him Grampa and threw themselves around his neck each chance they got, this little man with a lion's mane of white, and teeth still sparkling after 80 years. They brought him glasses chilled with tea, and dentures, cane, pillows, anything beyond the grasp of this precious man's knobbed and gnarled hands.

Precious, precious Mexican man they rarely saw, tucked in Guadalajara two thousand miles hence, his land, his old familiar land, far from flesh and blood that spoke english and bookended him wherever his body surrendered itself.

His days were brief, rising with sun and disappearing into shadowed rooms in afternoons. Just hours, mere hours to pat the children's heads, and kiss their hands, and rock them in his arms, and make them laugh with silly songs till tears dampened their cheeks, and his.

He ate in silence, his words often decimated with fog and fading pictures. But words are wisps that die in air, and he trembled when he gathered my children to kiss their foreheads, and his eyes clenched to stay strong, and my children heard the words he didn't say, and loved, loved, loved this precious, precious man.

VETERAN

His back's a toothpick stack racked with pain.
His legs are stone on hospice sheets in
Barstow, where VA nurses rub aspercreme
on his arthritic limbs, days melting like wax
one into the other, his 90-year-old eyes
opalescent murk.

His convalescent legs slog in midnight dreams
through devastated streets, Sicilian sky
lit bloody by rockets pulping
trenches filled with men he knew.
His sharpshooter fingers and eagle eyes
bring down krauts in trees in the Ardennes,
and krauts covered in branches to deceive his mark,
but he's the best.

His medals sleep in velvet trays in cedar drawers
now, room 356, because his shelf life tugs him
from pock-marked fields
to solitary rooms where walls
shimmy and run
like watercolors into smears.

ON JANUARY 1st, THE GLASS SLIPPER WON'T FIT*

all the horn-blowing confetti and
foam-belching bottles won't make a dent for
you cindy tho you walk along
The Route
among the million they say snuggled in sacks
barbecue pits glowing discard sofas warm with
cuddling card games skating guitarists balloons
in giant bouquets bobbing
in the chill

your chill sits squat in your heart your
legs lonely 'motons plodding you along
The Route
eyes blue china plates glazed cold
and when twelve comes you know
you know you know you just know
it won't matter she's still upstairs belching
blood bald head shriveled from the
keemo knobby body curled like a kidney
bean to ease the pain mom won't
get well

they kiss and sing and think
that final counted tick
counts her throat is sacked by renegades no
songs at home cindy no magic transformation at
the turning of the hands

---

* Painted on a large sign outside a Pasadena, California, house
  on New Year's Eve.

DEGAS

I have lost the thread of things.
I piled up my plans in a cupboard
for which I always had the key.
And now I've lost the key.
--Edgar Degas,
in a letter to a friend,
circa 1884

phlegm shrouds my eyes naked
models and I dance in the dust of my
studio sipping wine till sunbeams penetrate their
paleness too many women empty
bed I stroke them
onto the canvas

my salon fills with dark
suits for tea each after-
noon their women ruffled and laced with
bourgeois fantasies of me wild man of stories I passed

when they're all gone ripe breasts radiant
hair I slip into easel gardens of
Manet opera houses of Beraut gay streets
of Delacroix jumbled in pastel oil around my bed taking
me from gloom to worlds I once captured
in brilliance.

I STOPPED BY YOUR HOUSE

...today, Dorothea, and parked my car next to your curb overgrown with thistle and cockleburs. As far as I could see…decay and broken-hearted garden beds, solitary and denuded in unforgiving heat and missing you.

It's been a year since you slipped by the peach tree in the back and crawled for an hour to your door, thigh bone broken and bending and sweat beading your forehead and fingers, mud caking your dress and lips, neighbors deaf and blind as you crawled and hollered and hoped help would come from the heavens.

At the hospital, your leg was made straight that night, and your pastor sang optimism at your bedside, stroking your hands with holy certitude. But 90 years have a way of giving up, not fighting the good fight, and dissipating in a breath. And thus, as lightly as a candle's flame pinched shut, it was with you and death.

I walked your walkways in the height of noon today, and knelt by your favorite bed, dianthus and vincas nodding their dessicated heads, boughs entwined with one another for sustenance. Grasses gray, apples mere bits of wood in branches anemic with neglect, once-fertile soil lumped like stones beneath leaves curled and twisted from thirst. Oh, how your gardens hurt!

In the darkness of your porch, I touched your soul: the wooden, painted sign, *Peace on Earth*, your mantra in all your work, nailed securely to the post, evoking you, and teas we drank in shade, and your Quaker gentleness. I sat on concrete steps, in dust and webs, eyes closed, and smelled bouquets you once arranged in crystal vases by your door to brighten days of passersby and guests.

How lonely your house sits, windows cloudy and clapboard split, curtains gone and decorations stripped. How starved the flowers, petals faded, stems like stilts. Silence shrouds the front and rear, birds evicted, butterflies departed, bees frightened away by loss. Yet but a year, your joy was rooted in these.

I stopped by your house today, Dorothea, and grieved for nature you once loved, that loved you back, as we loved you, and you loved us. I stopped by your house and faced decay…but marveled at how memories obliterate the here and now and take us back with such resolve, to sights and sounds and smells and smiles and goodness and amity and peace.

I marveled at how memories prevail when the love is strong.

JANUS, THE GATEWAY GOD

You two-faced son of a gun, never in or out but
in-between, always in the path, in
doorways, portals, gates, wishy-washy wimp
not making up your mind. In or out? Always in
the way, immobile marble, looking front and back,
like a Mafioso marked for takedown. Wimp.

Anyone can straddle past and present, reliving
pain and glory, sneaking peeks at down the
road, wondering what boulders block our paths,
but staying put, stuck like heels in August asphalt,
like addicts zonked on sofas, trapped like
catatonic drunks who can't make up their minds.

You two-faced son of a gun, roman god they
say, but guarding doorways is what conspirators
do, their hands on secret knives, fingers on
lips, shushing, shushing, keeping the future under
wraps, not telling, not giving it away, killing us
with secrets. Hypocritic coward. Take a step
back, or lunge forward. Commit—make a move. Just
get out of the goddam way.

BY THE L.A. FREEWAY

1

Young black man, shirt stretched tight across his
shoulders, muscles undulating, lanky legs moving
suavely from car to car as he leans toward the glass,

as he offers anemic bouquets to drivers at the light, by
the ramp, who tap fingers at the sight of backed-up
cars on the concrete headache just above.

Too young to be freeloading, they say. Young
black man's white-teeth smile is supple, a band of light across
his dark. Too young, too healthy for sympathy, they
say and turn away. Should be throwing footballs at
the high school or the park,

should be throwing out his cardboard sign, grimy
hand-scrawled bit of corrugated crap that lies: "Please
help a vet. Hungry, sick."

He taps his black finger on rolled up windows, flashes his only
whiteness, smiles with lips pressed tight when driver after
driver at the light looks away and pretends he isn't there.

2

Young black man, prickly blanket spread between two
cans, lanky legs tucked beneath old sheets layered
on for warmth, candle in tuna tin shimmying near his arm,

offers bottle to the khaki man in sleeping bag,
his nighttime meal on a piece of rag pinned down with
stones as he fumbles in his pocket for a spoon.

Young black man's smile lies dark. Too young,
they'd said, too young to go, to fight, too young
to die so far away. Should be throwing footballs in
the college down the road instead. Sympathy wasted on
him then, absent now since who knows when.

His hand-scrawled sign lies face-up in a puddle
near his head. He coils his blanket like a jelly roll, discipline
remembered. Young black man vomits out his soul,

rubs his fingers on closed eyes, blotting out the day, the red
desert nights, rattles and shouts, then prays with lips pressed
tight, pretending he was never there.

COMING TO EMPTY

It's purpling time, the sun low above mountain ridges. My hand
      trembles with the front door key: for the first time in 19 years,
      silence awaits on the other side. My dog lay limp on linoleum
      at the vet's, her feathered tail curled as it did in pain, amber
      eyes wide, marbles glinting back the ceiling lights, fear and
      surprise at how rapidly she died.

I asked forgiveness as I stroked her fur, forgiveness for not letting
      go the month before, when she limped and fell and wheezed
      through midnight hours on the wooden floor. I held my Mica,
      cupped her head and praised her strength, her will, her
      loyalty, hanging on, holding on, though her body whimpered
      resignation.

I asked my Mica for forgiveness, swaddled her in the quilt she loved,
      carried her belated to my van like precious luggage. She
      panted on the floor, swollen tumors pressing, rippling up and
      down her back like stony paths. I asked my Mica for
      forgiveness as I knelt to hold her head while the needle
      pierced her hip.

At home, the stillness stabs. I gather Mica's things: her leash, and
      hang it on the closet hook, not ready yet to let it go. The pink
      child's brush with plastic tips I used to stroke her shoulders
      till her lids drooped shut. The heart-shaped ID tag she wore
      like a charm since just a pup. Her blue and white ceramic
      bowl on a rubber placemat by the sink. Just inside the kitchen
      door, a plastic bin filled to the brim with kibbles and organic
      treats for "senior vim and vigor." Mica's things.

I weep for Mica as I weep for me. We hang on to things like we hang on to life: afraid to see the end of purpose, afraid to phase out shards and broken bits, afraid to see how giving up is also love.

TO VANESSA*

your sweet face fooled us all, lulled us into
thinking a heart of milk and honey could stave
off monsters

your soft arms folded us in laughter, tricked
us into thinking your songs and crazy dancing
could castrate demons

your dreams consumed us— your films, poems,
music, art, scripts transporting us to
worlds you grew

but you buried truth in pillows, in journals
shut to daylight, in night clubs cramped with
sweat, malt liquors, smoke, and coke

you buried your soul in keyboards clacking
beyond sleep, churning your brain into
believing fame followed close

vanessa of visions huge, transcending blue-eyed
men who blocked, who slammed doors shut, who
could not see the world you were

vanessa of gentle eyes that wearied of the tug,
the pull, the pressing down, the clouds that hung
like lead around your soul

dreams die hard, you said the day before, but
we were lulled and tricked and blind and deaf and
never saw your spirit's death

---

* In memoriam: Vanessa Libertad Garcia, age 29.

REVUELTO CON ARROZ*

My grandfather
        was never sick a day in his life.
His wife
        can vouch for that.
        He used to wear a fuzzy cowboy hat
inside the house all the time, lying
        on the sofa, taking naps even.
        He was used to giving
my big brother and me his empty cloth Bull Durham Tobacco
        bags.
He'd put pennies in them, and my brother and me would brag
        to our buddies that Grampa
        was a rich man.
He was often mean
        to the neighbor kids, but it seems
        he had a soft spot for my brother and me.
We'd often be
        just, oh just sitting somewhere,
        in the kitchen or the porch, and Grampa'd pull up a
        rickety chair
and clap his hands, and stomp his feet, and sing out in his raspy
        voice:
        Howdy do my partner, revuelto con arroz!

It didn't make no sense to us,
        but it was just
the sight of him, smiling, clapping, dancing like a clown,
        his brown
leather-wrinkled skin crinkled with laughter
        after
he'd get us to jump up and join him in his silly game.

We'd clap hands, stomp our dusty feet along with him, and sing
        the same
        Howdy do my partner, revuelto con arroz!

What laws
        dictate that fun must have a point? Anyway,
        Grampa was never sick a day
in his life, till he had his heart attack and died.
My brother and I cried and cried
and hugged and kissed his hat and sat
        in a corner of his bed and sang without his raspy
        voice,
        Howdy do my partner, revuelto con arroz!

---

*   Literally: "How are you, my partner, mixed with rice!" It
    was a nonsense rhyme that my grandfather might have made up.

OSCAR THE BLADE RUNNER

You run on scimitars, slicing
grooves on tracks, stirring dust
with pumps of arms and stumps.
Hero muscles, olympian grit
churn miles alongside athletes whole,
pitting your heart against their calves and feet.

Oscar, how we loved your fire!
Loved your will to race the wind and stars,
to brace the weight of Afrika on blades,
re-calibrate what makes a man be god,
transform a newborn's curse to glory
for a boy denuded of his bones and limbs.

But she loved you, too, and you loved her.
You fired four times and the god in you
absconded in a blink.

How mighty is the fall of gods,
how swift their tumble from their pristine perch,
that proves to worshippers how
quickly
goodness
dies.

SYLVIA PLATH'S FINGERS

tucked the quilt
    around her son, coaxed his baby foot back
                         under safety

        stroked her daughter's curls,
            pulled blinds to blot the
                         wintry moon

filled a slip:
        her doctor's phone, his name

filled gaps 'round kitchen windows, door:
        tucked tea towels tight

turned her oven knob

        gripped the edges of the metal door,

                    bones white.

HAITI #1: BURIALS*

Bones lie crushed beneath concrete. Feet and fingers showed
      darkly here and there, moving days ago, silent now, dusted
      with powder.

Former elegance lies buried:
the Montana, with ornamental grilles, and ivy once
curling lovely on balustrades, and millionaire art
collections gloating in mansions
before devastation devoured leisure in a blink.

Haiti women and men rise each day, comb their hair, soothe
      rosary beads in Sacre Coeur.
Burials fill the hours of survivors driving trucks, dumping
      neighbors, brothers, sisters into dust
so deep and long.

---

* This poem was written shortly after the earthquake struck
  Haiti in 2010.

HAITI #2: A DROUGHT OF TEARS

"I'm crying in my head, but if I let
tears come out, they won't stop."
--Jean Exeme Lundy
Haiti translator*

Haiti fears to open the dams of mourning
after the monstrous split of earth.

Cry, Haiti: Holler redly in dusty air,
enumerate the bones you've hid.

Let scarring start in your bosom,
catharsis cupping your sorrow like hands.

---

* Reported in New York Times online,
  January 31, 2010.

HAITI #3: BELLY FAT

She sleeps three hours at a spurt, curled
in the corner where her cot once stood, nurse
uniform crumpled and grayed beyond hygiene.

Today she glimpsed a Red Cross visitor's magazine
lying glossy by the makeshift sink: *Ladies' Home Journal*,
pristine letters boasting, *"How to Beat Belly Fat."*

She skims this wisdom published in another world, for alien
beings with hands that move, that lift untainted food
to lips unparched, with hands encased in flesh that does not
hang in strips.

She gathers a teenaged mother lying among stones
outside the clinic door, a wisp of rags clinging to her baby, suckling
breasts gone dry, her ribs a cage that could not keep her breath secure,
her arms mere sticks that once cooked dirt for food.

Beneath the trees, corpses pile uncounted, diarrhea
drying out their souls and bellies, twig legs twisted by
cramps and covered with stench.

GHOST BIKES IN CHICAGO

1

I saw another one today, at
Fullerton and North, sprayed
white, stripped of its chain,
bedecked in flowers,
its hand-lettered sign,
Lizamarie Harris, taped to
the icy seat, and photographs
of a girl smiling wide, eyes
crinkled with promise.

Lizamarie: what was she
thinking, where was she going,
whom was she seeing,
what was she singing or whistling,
what did she carry in her
knapsack, how did she
fall and land, and did she
perish right away, or stare at
blue sky and listen to
birds whistle as she
waited to die?

Fullerton and North: cars
zip like drunken rats
in mazes and chutes, potholes
grab tires steaming with speed.
What was Lizamarie's killer
thinking, where was he going,

whom was he seeing,
what was he singing or texting,
what was he sipping from his
Starbucks cup, and did he
stop at the striking and run
out to see the young girl dying
and weep at what he'd done?

2

The first ghost bike
I ever saw sat sedate
below State and Wells,
a snowy, castrated frame
tied with twine to
the speed limit sign
glinting in the sun.
A twenty-something Asian
smiled from the handlebars,
assured and educated,
stacks of hardbacks in his arms,
De Paul on his cap,
the photo wounded by wind and chance.

Cursive epitaphs curled on
yellow post-it notes
taped to the seat
like improvised tombstones.
Happy birthday, they said,

and *We aced the final*
exam for you, Quan!
They loved him well.

3

To go out in the morning
with hope brimming in pockets,
backpack pregnant with plans,
young muscles pumping
toward places where dreams grow.
To taste wind and sun
and shade and rain and
know that pain is brief
and life lies long.

To look clear-eyed past fear,
to cycle past the roar and thunder
of hasty cars hurtling
with buses and Harleys
in criss-crossing lanes
unnervingly skinny and cramped.

To leave without saying goodbye,
without a prayer,
with life's loose ends
frazzled and
hanging limp.

DO NOT RESUSCITATE

a wrinkle in hospital sheets
      parchment
            mute

cellophane breast
      chilled   twig bones
                 stilled

mucus-eyes
      fading   breath
            clipped

TAHRIR SQUARE, CAIRO:
JANUARY 27, 2011

I sleep on cement under smoke from fires we
grew this afternoon and
crystalline stars that blink at us and
doubt we can prevail. They've lit these
skies far longer than the tyrant has
stolen light from us.

As far as eye can see, shoulders touch shoulders,
blanketed in wooly faith brought by sisters or
mothers who sit cocooned by kettles alight,
and whisper their hatred and grit. Even
women fight.

My brother's broken head almost quashed my
will, his eye twisted and shut in a
hole deep and dark. But he staggered to the
corner, where angels came from nowhere to
bandage bones and flesh, stanch the rivers of
red and men, these angels from the stars that
question. And the broken men staggered
back to barricades, to corrugated shields and
stones, to dignity as men,
unbroken.

Today, unbelievers on camels and horses
swooped like the apocalypse upon our empty hands,
whipping sticks and clubs, hurling fire in rags at
our mouths and eyes. Harout died, and three
others who awoke this day prepared for
death. When daylight comes,
it is my turn.

YOUR PYRAMID OF THE SUN

You clambered up monolithic stones like a spider on steroids,
twiggy girl of twelve, unafraid of how the heavens zoomed away the
more you climbed, earth cleaving from the sky.

Master of the ants below, you scanned Aztec fields, arms upraised
like priests with feathered knives approaching heaving chests
stripped bare for gods who watched.

Bending on one knee, your squinted eyes sought proof of sacrifice:
skinny channels carved in stones to carry blood away in rivulets,
obsidian figures cracked and lodged in crevices
that time forgot.

You lay on the platform at the top, stared for hours as clouds
raced past, the sun's heat baking stones, and thus, your back. Then:
Here is where they died, you said. *I feel their hurt.*

The sun slanted like stalks of wheat. You hugged your
knees on the pyramid's edge, a little girl reckoning in dust and
stones. *What sort of god needs pain?* you said.

You picked your steps precisely going down, head bowed, as
winds whipped dervishes around your feet and your hands trembled
on tiers of blocks flaring endlessly to earth.

MONSTER LADY

Who knew it would be like this?
Strong woman, monster lady, mover of *monoliths*,
she liked to say, not *mountains*, but *monoliths*.
Tough momma since thirteen: *monster lady*, she
called herself, woman who built our house, leather
hands cooking dinner for seven when the hammer stopped
pounding and the sky purpled. Tough cookie without
a man, welts hidden, legs scarred.

But in the end she moved molehills. Her brain dumped her,
one side crumpling, wetting, when the going got too tough
too long, the other side pumping her to *be strong*.
The wet one won.

With time, airy visitors came in pairs, perched in corners,
smirking in dusk. They took off their heads, she said, and
sat beneath her dining table. Her cloudy eyes shooed
them away, trembled when they moved near her wooden
knees. She cursed at them, tough momma, made them
know she wasn't ready.

Soon, others from a far-off time waited outside windows,
came brazen in daylight, stood by her stone hands,
floated above. These she'd truly loved. Her brain burst
one day in a wetness of recognition. Who could've known
she'd go this way? Who could've guessed love could
take out a monster?

THE MAYANS WERE WRONG

oh so very very wrong, those feathered prophets
dancing on monoliths while blood flowed down stones
and puddled in cobbled streets

the mayans were fooled, their cool calculations and
cocky calendars clicking along while galaxies
crashed and spun and showered them with word of death

oh those mayans were wrong, so very very wrong —
shamans and seers and mathematicians declaring us
dead on the heels of the 12's

spin on, spin on, pyramid doomsayers,
for we've won a reprieve, a decade more to tilt
at mills and hold our world together with tape

CROSSING

"People see scavengers... another human being has fallen.
We accept it as a way of life. You know it's going to keep on going on."
--Los Angeles Times, "Corridor of Death,"
June 23, 2013

1

a faded shirt impaled on brambles, shoes
tilted by the rutted road, laces caught with thorns
and webs, water jug crumpled and coated with sand.

the texas rancher wipes his brow, squints
into heat shimmying from dirt and rocks.   no
vultures, no wild hogs screeching and tearing at
flesh. this death is old.

he picks his way through scrub brush and mesquite,
dust swirls circling his boots.   he knows the body's
here, somewhere, somewhere close by—
more bones and desiccated flesh to count,
more human detritus to unearth and wonder over.

amazing how quickly dreams suck into themselves
and die, how bodies young a day before cannot survive
the push, the trek, how legs collapse among these brutal
stones and melt, how brothers let their kin give in, to
stay behind and perish under cactus and this satan sun.

2

"corridor of death" they call this god-forsaken swath
between borders and the end of dreams.   corridor

of death, where nations meld, vastness blurring one
side to the other, miles that beckon and destroy.

under tangled oaks, the rancher sees a hand,
bloated fingers curled, wedding band glinting in
shadow.   the man is shirtless, eyelashes matted
with dust, bare feet and thighs gnawed to the bone
by badgers and raccoons.

how quickly life snuffs out when promises betray, when
hopes collide with land that must be crossed, that must be
broken through, earth and dust and sand and stones and
thorns and sun and all the innocence that kills, when all this
must be crossed, and maybe dreams survive
on this other side.

but this death is old.
each death is old.
the rancher lost count so many years ago.

SHADES OF BLUE

Blue is black before the sun awakes, black swirled with
silver as light sneaks through, not fooling gods or
men. Come do your job, Blue. Bring all your brushes, throw
your strokes above our heads and all around and show us
what you have.

Paul Newman eyes. Blue of talent and compassion, his
blueness giving fortunes to the hungry, heart-bursting jeans
blue sexy in a streetcar, hustler, cool hand luke blueness.
When he died, blue eyes turned black, as sapphire tears fizzled
out and he took his blueness to the clouds.

Ocean blue slicked black with gushes from the deep, blue
smirched with orange, red, churning, burning, billows
black, hearts blue, suffocated hearts, drowned riggers in gulf
blue, blue grief, pelicans blue-black from tar and death, blue
eyes weeping at BP greed.

Pool blue respite in the Bronx, wavy concrete aqua heat,
crystal blue splashes, spindly children in red, brown, blue swimsuits,
dark eyes, blue eyes blinking, squinting, little lips blue from cold,
watchful mothers under blue canopies, under a cloudless sky blue
smug in its iron grip.

Blue, blue, you never come alone. You drag red along, for heartbreak,
black for night, loss, death, and grief, and white for heat and sky
gloves blue white. Blue swirls with silver, never fooling god or man,
blueness swirling high, deep, dry, wet, vast, small, bin laden's grave
and porcelain christ statue eyes.

NOT KNOWING

We huddled by the stove at midnight, two anxious women
whispering hurts at the end of a difficult day, your face puddled and
swollen, and you emptied your soul into my hands and told
me things I never knew had burnt your spirit. You told me things that
seared mine.

I never knew, I never knew these bonfires in your heart, my daughter,
but you say I did, and I weep till my throat is raw
and almost shut with grief and disbelief. How can this be.

Your lips swelled like ripe tomatoes, you say, under veils of
visitations and trips away. Your father's open hand struck like a
swinging gate across your cheeks once alone and you were little and
frightened of this man whose blood coursed in you, blood
that spoiled your weekend dresses.

How can this be. You assure me this is true. And you assure
me that I knew.

My kitchen bulb glares cold and you weep and I wrap my arms
around myself in disbelief and for decades you thought I didn't
care and I whimper, decades late, eons in arrears.

You dredge the scum that buried you and memory, that piled
like thieves against tall walls of stone to quash and strip
humanity till pain remained solitary and stolid, the thing you
knew for sure. The monster with your blood spilt yours in
rooms dark and distant, your childhood like a funeral train,
and me not knowing not knowing.

FLIGHT 93: SEPTEMBER 11, 2001

Each cloudy mile pulls us closer to our doom.
So near to Heaven, it's easy to forget how bound to earth we are:
Wives, babies, lovers, friends compel us to the ground,
our histories, our futures.

Red-banded madmen spill blood in these aisles, their monster
     brothers blowing black holes in our cities' hearts nearby.
Four madmen, coward blades slicing, momentarily subduing.
Four blindmen: focused on their targets, they cannot fathom our
     philadelphia that shatters our fear for selves.

We'll ice their thunder,
we'll ice their terror,
in the Pennsylvania fields rushing to embrace us.

TALISMANS

She spreads her talismans around our house:
Rocks shaped like hearts, from creek beds, backyards, lonesome alleys
      when she takes our dog around—stopping, starting, stooping,
      her fingers flicking dirt, unearthing treasure, her hearts.
Her talismans.

At home, stones rounded smooth like eggs fill bowls. Each place we
      sit, and take a breath, and catch a break from life, and
      remember how we were when young, her talismans repose:
Shells iridescent, sharp or crescent, large like helmets or conches
      furled unto themselves.
Bamboo platters piled with sand and bits of wood the waves spat up.
Pine cones nestled among curled orange rinds, their fragrance
      intertwined.
Petals sprinkled on the tablecloth, by beeswax candles and pedestals
      of pears.
Her talismans.

Her waning days are marked by garden walks, by sitting at the
      waterfall with songbirds in full tune, by lying silent in her
      hammock, counting stars.

Inside, she wafts from room through room, her bits of nature greeting
      her at every turn, to soothe, to keep her grounded to the dust,
      to sands, wind and sun, trees and rocks, the mighty and the
      small, all that she's been and will be again: the simple and the
      simply grand.

SGT. BOBBY BALES, AFGHANISTAN

Your wife blogs about her hero on the sands, while you drag your
bleeding foot five miles and steal peace from swaddled babies
sleeping at the bosom of their mothers.

Villagers are easy targets when it's black, when stars hide in clouds
and the moon hunkers down behind hellish mountains, and the
children curl together on blankets strewn on dirt, and elders set aside
their prayer beads to give their god a rest. Villagers are easy when
their shields are bony arms and nothing more.

We grieve for lives you took. Sixteen souls. Women with toddlers in
their clutch, or babe in womb, old men with dessicated bones
enwrapped in dust, sleep-eyed fathers with beards gone dry. Slicing,
shooting, maiming, burning, your robot soul desecrated theirs in this
god-forsaken land that forsook gods of every ilk for centuries. Your
robot boots took death from hut to hut, your veins entombed in ice as
you immolated
child after child,
elder after elder,
woman after woman
with hands steady as stone.

What did you do before this hellish night?
What did you do before devils sucked your spirit and your bloodlust
sought the village beds?
What did you do to barter death for hell, perdition for damnation,
your soul for purgatory?
Oh oh oh, Sgt. Bales, what did you do?

GRUMPY: THE UNTOLD STORY

He protested his name, but his six brothers pressed it
on him with paperhanger zeal soon after
his stump mother wheezed herself into eternity.

She was tucked into a hillside; his eyes swelled for seven
days til they seamed in drought. He knelt
for hours, kneecaps already huge from toiling in the
mines all day, and lambasted God. He plucked
briar-rose and honeysuckle on his way
from work; with sooty hands for years arranged
these on his mother's grave.

He had a lute, too—once. His smiling brother
burst the strings in temper. And once, near death,
he begged his Doc for aid but saw,
instead, the six march out—and in and out, day
after day, whistling their team song while he
coughed and spat in his cot-stench.

When *she* came along, he marvelled at her
length and how she touched him with fingers
gentle as his mother's. But it was late. The
assassination was complete.

TO MERCEDES IN LAREDO:
AN 88-YEAR-OLD POET

You once distilled poetry from cobwebs taut between your
       bougainvillea and the grapes.
Glassene drops shimmied in the morning cool, your
       breathless fingers touching them to anoint your lips.
The tinting of the sky with dawn would draw you,
       moth-like, from your satin quilts, could draw you, naked,
       to your jewel garden, where you hailed rose, camellia, lily,
       hibiscus, gardenia with reverence.
Each day your virgin-eyes relearned the sun, the air, the
       clouds, the slanting of the light in pools of gold
and shadows wet against the trees.

Your books lie quiet now, their songs consigned to dusk
       that clouds your days.
Your hands curl on the rattan chair, fingers stone that
       cannot move a pen or pluck a stem.
Outside, blooms that once inspired paeans curl and fall
       in piles.
Propped on pillows in your window bay, you gaze at
       grandeur that once was, your opalescent eyes
       recalling seasons, reasons, rhymes, and visions.

AFTER THE FINAL ACT

No curtain call for me.
When the drama's done,
I'll rush backstage
and seek you out.

You'll be there.
Our tears will be our "Bravo!"s
while we embrace our soulbodies
tightly in reunion,

and smile at the scenes I botched,
at my anemic lines of heroism,
my maudlin moments,
my final soliloquy of hope.

You played the script before
and left the boards many years ago
to sit backstage and wait for me.
You knew we'd meet once more.

And so we shall.
I'll set up residence backstage,
immortal neighbors, you and I,
after the final act.

III

...All of Us

GROWING UP DUSTY IN A SMALL TEXAS TOWN

Our ankles were always gray, caliche
dust swirling like guardian angels around twiggy brown
legs leaping potholes, tripping on dirt clods. Nine
children oblivious to what it meant to be growing up dusty.

In winter, rivers of mud separated us from Licha, Juan,
Susie. Dripping mesquite trees beckoned. Black puddles
dotted our 'hoodscape far as child eyes could see, little
lakes navigated house to house as we grew up dusty.

When morning light tickled our bedfaces, dervishes danced
through cracks and chinks in sills and walls and floors and doors.
Grandma's rag couldn't stem the tide of constant coats
of dust as we grew up in our small Texas town.

On the other end were asphalt roads, mown lawns and
children with patent leather shoes that stayed black.
At school, only chalkboard dust bound them and us as
we grew up dusty in our small Texas town.

QUILTS

Mother plugged up the coffee spout
      with foil after dinner
to keep the cockroaches out
      and laid a pile
of patchwork quilts on the chilly floor
      for us to sleep on and urinate.
She hung them on the doors
      next morning,
colorful, stinky banners hanging
      room through room
to dry—rearranging
      them next night so the most pissed
would be on the bottom of the stack
      and we could sleep without the stench
of too much wetness.

Her black
      coffee sometimes had a baby cockroach
drowned in its bitters. Got through the foil, I guess,
      damned little fool,
got through the plug to mess
      her brew, as we messed her quilts—
growing kids lying shoulder to shoulder
      on the floor,
growing older,
      still peeing, still wrapped in each other's arms
to keep warm.

OLD HABITS

How easy it is to forget
how old habits in the brain trick us,
trick us,
into thinking you're at my door,
or here in the kitchen by my side, sipping
at the mug, sighing at the early hour,
calling my name, your
mouth at my ear.
How easy, how easy.

The brain wipes away years, tears,
contorts memory to slave shadows of
itself, clipping connections to calendars
and seasons, children growing into
future mists we veil over when
we're tricked. I hear footsteps,
jingling keys, the gentle click
of a door unlocked, water lapping
at your washbowl, gentle, curling,
steaming stream gurgling, and
you humming as you shave your neck.

How easy it is
to hear these precious sounds again,
these tiny tunes of love, familiarity,
tricking death and me with
double shots of cruelty: warmth
swathing me at the reliving, the
unguarded glow from being tricked, then
stabs of recollection, of seeing you
lowered in the ground, mounds of
flowers sliding back into the dirt.

—

HUNGER

I can take the grumbles, the groans that gurgle in my stomach
morning, night, and long hours at my desk.
I can take my belly sticking to itself inside.
I can take this.
As a child in little texas towns, field to field, I learned that food is not
a given, work doesn't magically bring food, and some of us aren't
meant to eat as others do.
I can take this.

My father's back was black from sun, my mother's hands like broken
stone. My own were criss-crossed red from cotton bolls, sharp leaves,
and thorns.
Your hands weren't meant for pencils, mama said, *or for kissing,* papa
muttered as he sat on dirt at noon. But he pressed my fingers to his
lips, and smiled, and took a bite of bread.
I could take it, eating like birds, working like horses, pushing tired
bones.
We piled on quilts spread on the floor at night and hummed
grandmother's songs to stave our hunger.
We all took it, stripped of hearts but beating on.

But my children are a different test.
They look out dusty glass on windows high above the street, chicago
lights just twinkling on in shops and sidewalks far below, the long
night just unwinding.
My boy and girl have drunk their cup of milk, and eaten the
sandwich they split.
I gave them crackers in cellophane I picked up at the deli kiosk at my
job.
They lie like urchins in my bed, two stowaways with legs entwined
like twigs, bellies grumbling under the blanket that used to be mine.

—   —

88

When our room is black and still, neons blinking half a block away, with alley drunks passed out below, I wonder at the world.
I wonder at this world, at how it takes and takes and takes, at how our bones can break in toil, and our hearts collapse, and our spirits dessicate, without a murmur of protest.

I wonder at this world, at how children lie in cribs, or sit at desks, or lean on stoops with bellies vacant and souls the same, and how the world goes on.
I can take it, for myself.
I can take it.
But children…children…oh, children.

ON LOAN

Listen, my son, you were never truly *mine*
and I not *yours*.
We've been on loan to one another,
don't you know. All of us are thus: lent
out, like a condo you lease for years and live
in and love and invest in and vacate someday.
Nothing keeps.

My womb was irrevocable house for you, a ghost
umbilicus on you even as I speak. You're so
much in my heart that tears spring
uninvited on the road, at my desk, in my books when
I think of how you've grown
away. Manhood hastens termination.
The lease will end.

At bedside, you swath my hand, put on
your bravest face, recount
your childhood to cheer me with the thought of how
close we've been. The needles do not hurt like
this. For twenty years you've been my sun,
my blue, blue sky, my stars in velvet, my
raison. I may vacate tomorrow, or the next or next.

What giant risks we take! To know
what fluff life is, ephemeral tethers, yet
to bind heart to heart, hanging on, on
loan, on lease, to leave, to lose.
Loss cuts deeply when there's so much love.

IT'S MIDNIGHT

and I've tiptoed to windows black, to gaze beyond
treetops at the milk-moon, ensconced among
fluff and shards, where we'll all be someday: so
high, so high, so chilled, alone, almighty, small,
remembered and forgotten.

wee hours kill and soothe, detritus of the day just
dead, darkness portending what lies ahead, comfort
rationed in swaths of silence.

wee hours tug me to this glass, to hallways
lined with faces ancient and somber in
vigil, faces lost to decades of dust, awakened
at midnight with me and the moon so high and
round and unattached.

ANNIE'S LAP

Moonlight slants onto the rocker, lights
up the woolen throw on Annie's
lap, caresses baby's cheek as they
both sit cocooned in the old chair by
the window.

Quiet, quiet, just the gentle
crick-crick of the rocking, rocking,
rocking, baby's breath soft spurts of
sweetness on his mother's breast, Annie's
eyes at rest for now,

for the moment,
for this space of silence,
for this precious blink of peace.

Light years above their heads, stars
explode in inferno bursts of chaos, blackness
sucking into heaviness, rocks hurtling
violence across galaxies, cosmos tilting,
crashing, ricocheting in vastness uncontrolled
by deity or man.

Outside her window, moonbeams light up
Annie's porch, and diamonds arc above her
roof into darkness tall and calm, shimmying, glimmering

in this moment,
in this space of silence,
in this precious blink of peace.

CLUTTER, MENTAL CLUTTER

All the shoulda's, coulda's of the day crowd
in these wee hours: clutter,
mental clutter

swirling to stop sleep, piling tall in
corners, layering guilt for
tasks undone—stories unbirthed, blogs musty with
last month's breath, emails stacking like
cut stone.

Clutter, clutter, mental clutter—
unforgiving, scraping on the backs of eyelids
raw and opened big. Blackness
reigns from wall to wall around my bed, but
clutter calls me out,
chastises like a whip, keeping
sleep at bay and
my body
crucified and still.

THE UNDIVORCED

Alfred J. Prufrock spoke of measuring
life out in coffee spoons. We ration
ours in thimbles and don't seem to mind.

How can passion flatten into slippers
old, worn thin and colorless, shushing along
our wooden floors, squashed silent?

But we plod on, sitting abreast in
church pews, sharing hymnals and
prayers and holy charades.

You go your way and I mine. You
fade into your office walls, and cable shows,
blogs, ebay, and coffee shops.

I lose myself in backyard bowers, take
garden tours with women twice my
age, recalling bouquets you used to give.

We used to dance on the rooftop of
the Bluezz Club, and sleep on a mattress
dragged outdoors in summer months.

You used to transport me with
touch, with songs crooned into my
ears till our eyes closed in bliss.

We used to lie entangled, legs caressing,
whispering in darkness about our day,
but who remembers all that now?

Most often, we are proverbial ships.
My nights are your days, and for years I've
slipped like stone, alone, into my side of bed.

WHAT DO I RACE AGAINST?

what do i race against
    a blankened slot
             empty lane
i wasn't ever here

    to be cinder on a track
or worse   the absent breeze
            on oven days

no no-shows
     the race must run
    i'm here to put on a good show folks

there's something here
    little puddle of pride
   sometime water knees   brittle feet
but that puddle

      oh that puddle

NEIGHBOR LADY ON THE FRONT PORCH

Perhaps if I pile my dreams on a plate and offer them
up, I won't reckon them much.
Tomorrow I'll hang my soul out on the line
and pin it tidy with wooden clothespins
so even though the wind blusters, my soul won't fly.
Tonight—well, tonight, I'll open up the matchstick gate
and pluck my heart out like a ripe plum and
stash it in the broken drawer by my bed.

Yes.
One by one I'll give them up.
My mind I'll lay on the backstoop with the dog dish and
maybe he'll lap it up and swallow it whole.

Yes. And then I won't have anything to lose.
You'll wonder why I sit content on my porch all day, and
rockrockrock, backandforthbackandforth, like a perfect
clock, and you'll pass by and envy me,
envy old Wanda, everyone envying me,
for not having a care in the world.

AWAKE

*"Leslie Gamble says he spent 12 years without
a wink of sleep. Gamble was hit by a truck. After
the accident, he lost fragments of memory—and
stayed permanently awake."*
--From OMNI Magazine

Sheep long ago gave way to zebras, snakes, and geese
loping, slithering, honking in paths of booming
trucks.

I phone empty offices at one
and count the rings, spill
to phantom businessmen my schemes
for putting zippers in jock straps
and drinking quinine to lose weight.
I stalk chill streets, confide to corner
bums that I'm a spy. I
sing to doorknobs, rattle ten or twelve, climb
elms and iron ladders till my fingers bleed.

I pray at curbs. Tenth and Marley lie
like death at three
with asphalt trash lit redly under
neon lights that stay awake with me.

At home books die and flutter to the floor
when desert eyes can take no more.

BITTEN TONGUE

Teeth clamp on feisty flesh,
wrestle with truth or opinions hurtling
from slippery corners of our mouths.

We want to be ourselves,
speak unvarnished words, lay open
dusty volumes of thoughts locked up.
We're friends.
Friends forgive blithe slanders,
saucy slips of tongues,
        don't they?

Oh, the red pain of bitten tongue,
sliding back, limp, silent in slickness,
hiding behind closed teeth, sewn lips,
saving grace, saving sanity,
sacrificing speech
        like lambs.

ROMEO & JULIET: HOW IT COULD'VE BEEN

They were children of hate—hate for one
another's kin, Capulets and Montagues killing
for decades without knowing why. When blood first soaked
the ground between his sword, and his sword, and the
mob swirled round the one and the other, daggers slicing
summer heat, curses roiling, dust enveloping their
capes and plumes and silk nobility, war was planted
square in their hearts and reason fled.

Decades of death paved the path for Romeo to
pick up the feud. But Juliet's gentle cheek and satin
eyes quashed his fight. Young Montague and Capulet felt
love, felt peace, and hope fluttered its frail wings about
their heads.

They spurned the public square, ring
of fights and deaths, and stole straight to a friar unafraid
of politics: Not Lawrence. Someone stronger, who bonded
them with surety, then took them straight to their
kinsman, man of power and steel, man who cursed the hate,
man who brought the force of law to Verona: their
Prince, awed by Romeo's and Juliet's chaste devotion.

Noble summonses flew like eagles' wings to castles Capulet
and Montague. Verona's fiery hand clamped down their
gangbattles, forced amity into their throats, and they
spoke amity. One by one, swords clattered to cobblestones,
scabbards untied from macho waists, fiery tongues
silenced.

Miles and miles away, in village unnamed, sent on their
wedding night into the inky roads, prefacing princely ·
intervention, Romeo and Juliet birthed
their child of peace.

EARLY MORNING

She wasn't supposed to die across the
sunbeams, flowered night-
gown twisted around crumpled knees, eyes
widely unaware and questioning.

She wasn't supposed to die while
her coffeepot called, and toast rose
with a gentle click as she
cajoled and roused sleeping children.

She wasn't supposed to die while
she sang to the terrier licking her ankles,
and her husband ambled to her for their
morning kiss, white coffee mug ready for his brew.

She wasn't supposed to die like this,
arms around his neck, lips pressed to his ear,
warm breath gearing up for morning talk,
her head tilting back to tell him something monumental.

But she died a lightning death, her
big heart failing, her body falling in an instant to
the sunlit floor, her mouth circled in pain, her hands
clutching her breast as her children walked in.

No guarantees. There are no guarantees in life, we've
been told and retold. Grab love, fight loss, find
joy, hang on, believe, and tell yourself again and again
and again that this day, *each day,* is irretrievable.

RAINY DAY IN 'NAM*

Dear God, the soldier says, then starts again:
*Dear God...*but can't proceed.

Rain bounces off palm fronds and strikes his eyes.
Drumroll rain renders earth a sponge.
Red bursts of death fan across rice fields swathed in mist,
while the soldier folds himself into a trembling ball
beneath the trees and moans for lack of prayer.
There is no purgatory, no limbo, no hell.
This war scorches the soul, cremates a man's spirit
quicker than flames.

The rain grows thicker.
He saw his death last night, a simple, simple horror:
he walked point-man along the humid trail
and a shadow from the trees fired into his skull,
the bullet boring through the other side,
the soldier falling limp,
bloodied eyes wide.

It was too real, too sharp,
and now pain again
overwhelms
as he weeps,
accompanied by the thrumming rain.

---

* In memory of my brother Danny Tellez, KIA in Vietnam, 1968.

DARK-MUSTACHIOED MAN

The dreamy, dark-mustachioed man
seemed a sculpture, his Valentino face chiseled
and somber in the shadow of potted palms where
the bistro walls met. He might have been in
silver-studded velvet astride a stallion, reins
firmly in hand, sweeping a Marquesa into
his arms, fleeing the hacienda for their
nightly tryst under the sultry moon.

But he moved, broke his pose.
The dark-mustachioed man
strode to a vacated table,
wiped it clean in three swift strokes,
then shrugged, wet rag in hand,
"I no speak English,"
when a bristle-faced patron in a flowered shirt,
large sweat stains under his armpits,
asked him where the men's room was,
then grunted at the ignorance of Meskins.

JUMPER

past 14 balconies and no one saw her
arms flung like a flapless bird's
head tossed back   eyes closed peace-
fully unto the clouds
like she always told the whitecoats she
would go

like this she'd say   and lay her alabaster
head in the void beyond her rail   frail
convalescent gown teasing the wind   *like this,*
with this box she'd say stepping light-
ly on a crate beside her feet

and no one heard her

when she hit
disjointed asphalt doll askew rubber face with
lips and nothing more   pieces gathered by
the bluecoats   flashlights scouring immense red
hoses washing the last of her away

HOW COULD YOU HAVE DONE THIS?

How could you
    How could you have
        How could you have done this,

Phillip Markoff,
    Craigslist Jekyll with a bookish gun,
    Gray's Anatomy ultimate lesson in death.

Golden boy with Harrison Ford
    smile, hiding blackness,
you golden boy, star over Boston,
    over stars that only flickered in your shadows.

Phillip Markoff
    with the shoelace throat.
    Wide-eyed hooker bound
    in your spell, your legs spreading hers, tying
    her wrists with terror,
shadow man,
    shadow boy with healing hands.

How could you
    How could you have
        How could you have done this,

Phillip Markoff,
    Craigslist Hyde with hubris deep and
    wide, your mom and dad with crystal
    wine regaling friends with tales of their fine
    son, and his Hippocratic vows,
the future filled with saving lives,
    and a loving wife.

By night, you bludgeoned a girl
     and shot her thrice.
By day the sun could not outshine
     your gentle ways, the keenness of your mind
     setting you atop your class, nice, golden boy.
Hypocritic man, shadow man,
     whose hands killed, and killed again.

MANKIND, LOVEKIND
(With Apologies to Walt Whitman)

Can't I be more than one?
Can't I be less than wife and mother, peel off my respectability
        for mankind, lovekind?
I want to brush your bodies with my warmth.
I do not have to know you.
Let me take your hand, press it to my mouth, anoint it with my tears
and lips.

I see you lonely in the lemon-light of street lamps, waiting collar-up
        against the chill.
I want my fingertips to brush your cheeks, my hand to grasp yours
        Whitmanesque.
Let me cuddle with you in your skinny bunk on cold nights, to
        share the prickly thinness of your blanket.
Let me laugh in your throat, feel the joy vibrate from your body
        to mine,
flesh-to-flesh, creating fluid Us-ness: *caritas – charité*.

Forget your plastic lunches in your hotel room.
Come eat the ripeness of my meal.
Blot out your echoing walls and let me fill your consciousness
        with my whispered feasts.
I want to meld into you, all of you, to dissolve into your beings,
        banish eternal longing to nothingness, pushing it,
        pushing it with my chaste heat to Tartarus.

ICONOCLAST

Trapped within the pinch of death,
you churn out one plastic moment at a time,
an organ grinder on a disjointed corner.

Iconoclast. Yesterday you cashed your paycheck,
      walked a dusky street and fed your bills
      to strangers while they laughed at you,
      but you pressed the paper in their palms,
      yourinsistenceoverwhelmingthem,

your cupboards bleak and cold.

Today your weary fingers soothed rosary beads,
      but now you sweat and lurch in another
      man's bed while your husband weeps at
      home, weeps for the virgin you've been to
      him these twenty years.

Iconoclast—to pass heaven for hell,
to barter death for death.

LAST RITES

Run your tongue
          round my breasts
How full of sex they are
swollen beneath your fingers your
mouth feasting on them   strange
darkness of your skin a
shadow on my sheets

Less a woman my lover said last
week less a woman   but
    your quivering fingers stroke my
      breasts hold them to your
lust your lips tracing silver
circles across their warmth

  You know they'll die
tomorrow   sliced coolly by stranger
          hands, pulled calmly by gloved
fingers onto the tray   bandages
wrapped flat against my
          chest a child
                              again a child again.

THIS I KNOW

the man at the head is not the
    head beautiful women have calloused
            hands the blind cannot forget what they've
    seen the deaf hear us loud and clear children
    lead the world priests and pastors mullahs
and rabbis are empty insanity is truth and
            truth is insane

we seek formulas and maps to shape our
    humanity squander eyes bury voice squelch
instinct and know more about facebook videos screens
            texts cars clothes cocktails malls and
        superficial things that distract derail mislead to
take us off the road the frontier is inside

and misunderstood forgotten blended in with
lands we navigate thinking this is the territory to
            explore and learn and we're off
            the road and blind and deaf and dumb until
        years piled in corners to the rafters help us peel
away layer by layer trivialities that sidelined wisdom and
            humanity that made us reach this point not
        knowing still not
                    knowing what it's all about

ABOUT THE AUTHOR

Thelma T. Reyna's poetry chapbook, *Hearts in Common*, was deemed a semifinalist in a national poetry competition, as was her first chapbook, *Breath & Bone*. Reyna is also author of *The Heavens Weep for Us and Other Stories*, winner of four national awards.

Her stories, poems, essays, articles, book reviews, and other nonfiction have appeared in journals, textbooks, anthologies, blogs, and regional media. She writes two blogs and has been a guest blogger on three others.

In April 2014, Reyna was named Poet Laureate of the Altadena (CA) Library District, a position she will hold for two years. She was also awarded a Most Inspirational Award for her accomplishments as an author and businesswoman by her State District Legislators in 2011.

Reyna is an editor and writing consultant with her business, The Writing Pros, and holds a Ph.D. from UCLA. Contact her at www.ThelmaReyna.com .

www.ingramcontent.com/pod-product-compliance
Lightning Source LLC
Chambersburg PA
CBHW051815040426
42446CB00007B/681